GEORGIA
The Empire State of the South

★

TEN TOP FACTS ABOUT GEORGIA

★ ★ ★ ★ ★ ★ ★ ★ ★ ★ ★ ★ ★

•State nicknames:	Empire State of the South, Peach State, Goober State
•State motto:	Wisdom, Justice, Moderation
•Capital:	Atlanta
•Area:	58,930 square miles
•State flower:	Cherokee rose
•State tree:	Live oak
•State bird:	Brown thrasher
•State insect:	Honeybee
•State marine mammal:	Right whale
•State song:	"Georgia on My Mind"

For Adam and Scott — my favorite southerners
— NEK

p. 4: U.S. Mint; p. 5: (left) Superstock Images, Jacksonville, FL, (right) North Wind Picture Archives, Alfred, ME, (bottom) North Wind Picture Archives; p. 6: (left) International Portrait Gallery, (right) North Wind Picture Archives; p. 7: Bettman/Corbis, New York, NY; p. 8: North Wind Picture Archives; p. 9: (left) North Wind Picture Archives, (right and bottom) Superstock Images; p. 10: Culver Pictures, Inc., New York, NY; p. 11(top) Superstock Images, (bottom) Bettman/Corbis; p. 12: (left) Library of Congress, (right, top and bottom) North Wind Picture Archives; p. 13: (top) Scholastic Photo Archives, (center and bottom) Bettman/Corbis; p. 14: Bettman/Corbis; p. 15: (top and bottom) AP/Wide World Photos; p. 16: (left) N. Carter/North Wind Picture Archives, (right) Superstock Images; p. 17: Superstock Images; p. 18: (top left) Corbis, (top right) R. Gehman/Bettman/Corbis, (bottom right) G. Rowell/Bettman/Corbis; p. 19: (top left) R. Gehman/Bettman/Corbis, (bottom left and right)Kelly-Mooney Photography/Bettman/Corbis; p. 20: (top left) D. Muench/Bettman/Corbis; p. 20: (center) D. Muench/Bettman/Corbis, (bottom) R. Gehman/Bettman/Corbis; p. 21: (top left) W. Bake/Bettman/Corbis, (bottom left and right) Superstock Images; p. 22: Bettman/Corbis (Berry), Superstock Images (Carter), Superstock Images (Cobb), Superstock Images (King); p. 23: Bettman/Corbis (Low), Bettman/Corbis (Mitchell); p. 24: AP/Wide World Photos (Robinson), M. Gerber/Bettman/Corbis (Turner), R. Rotolo/Bettman/Corbis (Walker); p. 27: North Wind Picture Archives.

All other illustrations by John Speirs

ISBN 0-439-22210-9

THE
Jim Henson
—COMPANY—

12 11 10 9 8 7 6 5 4 3 2 1   0 1 2 3 4 5/0

Designed by Madalina Stefan

Printed in the USA
First Scholastic printing, December 2000

GEORGIA
The Empire State of the South

By Nancy Krulik

SCHOLASTIC INC.
New York   Toronto   London   Auckland   Sydney   Mexico City   New Delhi   Hong Kong

A Celebration of the Fifty States

★ ★ ★ ★ ★ ★ ★ ★ ★ ★ ★ ★

In January 1999, the U.S. Mint started an ambitious ten-year program to commemorate each of the fifty United States. Over the next several years (through 2008), they will issue five newly designed quarters each year.

One side (obverse) of each new quarter will display the profile of George Washington and the words *Liberty, In God We Trust,* and *United States of America.* The other side (reverse) will feature a design honoring a specific state's unique history, the year it became a state, the year of the quarter's issue, and the words *E Pluribus Unum* (Latin for "from many, one"). The quarters are being issued in the order in which the states joined the union, beginning with the thirteen original colonies.

To find out more about the 50 State Quarters™ Program, visit the official U.S. Mint Web site at *www.usmint.gov.*

GEORGIA'S QUARTER:
The Sweetest Peach

Have you ever eaten a Georgia peach? Large, sweet, and unforgettable, peaches have come to represent the state of Georgia — and not just because so many of them are grown there. Many people feel that the sweetness of the fruit represents the personalities of Georgia's natives. After all, Georgia-style southern hospitality is famous worldwide.

So it should come as no surprise that the quarter design for the "Peach State" (as it is often referred to) features a huge Georgia peach in the center. The peach is surrounded by a silhouette of the state with a border made of live oak sprigs, representing the Georgia state tree. The banner above the peach bears the state motto: "Wisdom, Justice, Moderation."

In the Beginning

Long before the first European settlers arrived in what is now known as Georgia, this lush, mountainous land was home to thousands of Native Americans. The Creek Indian tribes made the southern part of the state their home, and the Cherokee lived in the north.

Hernando de Soto

The first European to visit Georgia was a Spanish explorer named Hernando de Soto. He came through the area in 1540 with several hundred men, searching for gold. Although he died without finding it, the Spanish, along with the French and English, all made claims upon the land over the next two centuries. In 1565, King Philip II of Spain sent an army, led by Pedro Menéndez de Avilés, to build forts along the Atlantic coast to keep the French from claiming the land. The first fort was built in what is now St. Augustine, Florida. The second fort was built on Saint Catherine's Island, Georgia, and a mission was established there, making this the first European settlement in the area.

Pedro Menéndez de Avilés

Explorers coming to the New World

Almost immediately after arriving in Georgia, Franciscan monks from Spain tried to convert the Native Americans to the Spanish way of life, completely ignoring the fact that they already had their own religion, language, and customs. Over the next century, the Indians engaged in many conflicts with the Spanish, French, and English. With the help of some Indian allies, the British managed to drive the Spanish out of Georgia by 1686. Throughout the next half century, however, the Spanish continued to try to regain control of the land.

In 1732, James Oglethorpe, a member of British Parliament, wanted to establish a colony in the area. Oglethorpe served on a committee that studied poverty in Great Britain. Back then, people who owed money were often sent to debtors' prisons where the conditions were very harsh. James Oglethorpe felt that debtors would have a better chance at a fresh start

Map of Savannah, 1742

by moving to the New World where they could work — producing wines, silks, and spices to be sold back in England. There were already many financially successful British colonies in America, including those in New England, New York, New Jersey, Pennsylvania, Maryland, Virginia, and the Carolinas.

Although the British government disliked the idea of a debtors' colony, King George II was eager to have more land in the area. He felt that the land's strategic position would help protect Britain's South Carolina from the French in Louisiana and the Spanish in Florida. The king granted Oglethorpe a charter to establish the new colony, to be named Georgia in honor of the king.

James Oglethorpe

Yamacraw Indians greeting Oglethorpe and colonists

In November 1732, James Oglethorpe and a boatload of more than one hundred immigrants set sail for the New World. After landing in South Carolina, Oglethorpe went off to look for the best spot to start his colony. He made his way up the Savannah River and met a group of friendly Indians at Yamacraw Bluff. The Indian leader ceded the land to Oglethorpe, welcoming the idea of a peaceful colony. Oglethorpe returned with the other colonists and built a town near the mouth of the Savannah River, naming it Savannah. A few years later, he settled the town of Augusta farther north along the river.

More than four thousand settlers from all over Europe came to Georgia during the next several years. The new settlers continued to be met with resistance from the Spanish in the south. In 1742, James Oglethorpe led British troops in a fight against the Spanish called the Battle of Bloody Marsh; a decisive victory by the British brought an end to the Spanish attempts to take over Georgia.

When Oglethorpe first started the colony, each immigrant received a certain amount of land for which he was responsible and from which he was expected to support himself. The land could not be sold or leased, and slavery was illegal. Eventually the colonists' request to allow slavery was granted by the charter's trustees, and in 1752 the trustees turned over administration of the colony to King George II, who appointed a royal governor, James Wright, two years later.

Joining the Revolution

Georgia's farmers were prosperous during the mid-1700s, and many of them were happy with British rule. Georgia depended more than any of the other colonies on financial aid and protection from Great Britain. James Wright was an effective administrator who was able to negotiate with the Indians for land and with the British royal government for money. For that reason, Georgians believed that British rule was to their advantage and the colony was not a leader in the movement for democracy. In fact, Georgia was the only one of the original thirteen colonies that did not send any representatives to the First Continental Congress, which met in Philadelphia on September 5, 1774.

But by 1776 the revolutionary fever that had been spreading throughout the northern colonies made its way to Georgia. Before long, a large segment of the population wanted independence, and the members of the colony agreed to send representatives to the Second Continental Congress. Georgians Button Gwinnett, Lyman Hall, and George Walton traveled to Philadelphia to sign the Declaration of Independence as representatives of their colony.

The first battle of the Revolutionary War to be fought in Georgia occurred in March 1776, when the British tried to take control of eleven rice boats in the Savannah harbor. The Georgians fought them off, and the British only captured two of the ships. In 1778, however, the British got their revenge and took over all of Savannah. Determined to hang on to a land as profitable as Georgia, they controlled almost the entire state by 1779. Finally, in 1782, American troops forced the British out of Georgia once and for all. On January 2, 1788, Georgia's legislature voted to adopt the U.S. Constitution and became the fourth state in the Union.

British attack on the harbor, 1776

Gold and Tears

In 1828, almost three hundred years after Hernando de Soto first searched for his fortune, gold was discovered in Georgia. Suddenly, thousands and thousands of people swarmed into the state with dreams of becoming wealthy. All those gold miners and their families needed somewhere to live, but there wasn't enough room for all of them.

Striking gold in Dahlonega

In 1830, the U.S. government came up with a way to free up more land in Georgia. The Congress passed the Indian Removal Act, which allowed the states to move the Indians from the land they were living on.

Although the legality of the act was argued in the courts for many years, in 1838 President Andrew Jackson gave the order to begin the removal of the

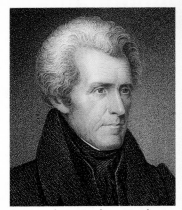

President Andrew Jackson

Cherokee people from their native land in Georgia.

Cherokee men, women, and children were ordered by U.S. army commanders to march thousands of miles from Georgia to what is now Oklahoma. The soldiers were not particularly concerned with the well-being of the Cherokee people, and the Native Americans were not provided with enough food or water for everyone to make the journey safely. Nearly four thousand Cherokee are believed to have died while walking what came to be called the Trail of Tears.

Cherokees leaving Georgia on the Trail of Tears

Slaves picking cotton

March to the Sea

While the promise of gold brought many settlers to Georgia, it was cotton that ultimately made many Georgians wealthy. With cotton as the major crop in the state, Georgia's early economy depended on the cotton-growing business — and that cotton-growing business depended on slavery. It was African slaves and their American-born descendants who toiled for hours in the hot Georgia sun picking bales of cotton.

For almost as long as there had been a United States, there had been cries from Northerners to outlaw slavery in all of the country. But the Southern farmers who had learned to depend on slaves to keep their businesses profitable objected.

In the mid-1800s, the disagreement between the states finally came to a head. The people of Georgia knew that the nation's new president, Abraham Lincoln, was against slavery. To Georgians and other Southerners, the message had become clear — if the Southern states remained part of the Union, their use of slave labor would become illegal.

Governor Joseph Brown led the movement for Georgia to secede (break away) from the United States. Georgians voted on the issue and, as expected, a majority wanted to leave the Union. On January 19, 1861, Georgia became the fifth Southern state to secede.

Although there are many reasons the Civil War started, it was the issue of slavery that brought out the strongest reactions in people on both sides. The Northerners were determined to abolish the practice, and the Southerners were just as determined to retain it.

Once the Civil War began, Georgia provided large numbers of troops for the Confederate army. The Confederates won the first Civil War battle fought in Georgia — the September 1863 Battle of

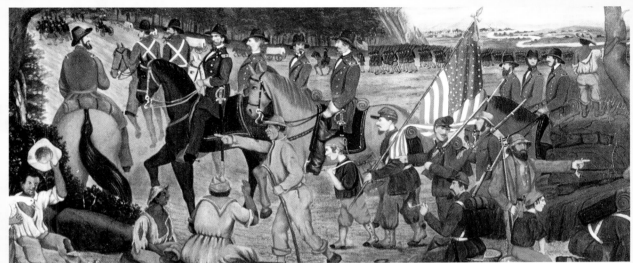

Sherman's march through Georgia

Chickamauga. Eight months later, however, General William Tecumseh Sherman led Union troops into the state, where they burned down much of Atlanta and then continued to demolish factories, ammunition works, and railroads throughout Georgia, not stopping until they reached Savannah. During this famous "March to the Sea," the Union soldiers also stole food and personal items from the plantations that lay along their path. By the time General Sherman had reached Savannah, more than one hundred million dollars worth of Georgia's property had been destroyed.

The Battle of Chickamauga

Buildings in Atlanta at the end of the Civil War

Reconstruction

The Civil War ended in 1865. Over the next several years, Congress debated what was required from the Confederate states in order for them to be readmitted to the Union. Eventually, three new amendments to the Constitution were written and the Southern states had to ratify all of them in order to become part of the United States again. The Thirteenth Amendment abolished slavery, the Fourteenth Amendment gave former slaves citizenship and stated that all men had equal rights, and the Fifteenth Amendment gave men of all races the right to vote. By 1870, all the former Confederate states had ratified the amendments and were readmitted to the Union.

Life for people in Georgia wasn't easy in the years immediately following the Civil War. Much of the state had been burned to the ground and needed to be completely rebuilt. Despite the destruction of their property, Georgians were able to reconstruct their railway systems and rebuild their cities and farms. By the turn of the century, farmers were growing crops other than cotton, including corn, peaches, tobacco, and peanuts. Industry was also growing rapidly. When the United States entered World War I in 1917, Georgia's factories were a major source of textiles and other materials needed by the U.S. army. Once again, Georgia's economy was booming.

Packing peaches at an orchard in the 1890s

Bales of cotton

Cotton plant damaged by boll weevil beetles

Attack of the Boll Weevils

Although Georgians were able to rebuild their land after Union soldiers had destroyed it, they still had to fight the forces of nature. During the early 1920s, cotton-eating boll weevil beetles invaded the state. Many farmers lost their crops — and their farms. As if that weren't a big enough blow to Georgia's economy, the Great Depression struck in 1929. As in most places in the country, many of Georgia's factories were shut down, and more Georgians found themselves out of work.

When the United States entered World War II in 1941, Georgia found relief. Suddenly, the army needed Georgia's farms and factories. Georgians went back to work in record numbers. Army bases opened all over the state, and Georgian men did their best to help the war effort — more than 325,000 of them served in the U.S. armed forces during World War II.

Soldiers training at Fort Benning during World War II

Practice attack at Fort Benning, 1945

Segregated water fountain

Let Freedom Ring

Georgia's economy may have become stronger during the 1940s and 1950s, but all the money in the world couldn't hide the fact that Georgia, like many states, had racial problems. One of the biggest problems was segregation — the separation of blacks and whites by law. Black children were not allowed to attend the same schools as white children. Many of the schools for black children didn't have enough supplies for all the students, and often the buildings were in poor condition. To help solve that problem, the U.S. Supreme Court outlawed segregation in public schools nationwide in 1954.

However, segregation was something southern whites had always lived with, and they were resistant to the change. Some white legislators even passed a law allowing the state to give money to private schools just to keep segregation alive. Finally, in 1961, Georgia's schools slowly began to integrate.

To help Georgia and other states continue on their path toward racial equality, the Southern Christian Leadership Conference, a civil rights group led by Dr. Martin Luther King Jr., an Atlanta-born minister, established its national headquarters in Georgia's capital. Dr. King believed in nonviolent protests and helped stage peaceful sit-ins and boycotts all over the state to deliver his message of equal rights for blacks.

Integrating schools by busing children

In 1964, Congress passed the Civil Rights Act, ending segregation in all public places. Racial discrimination didn't disappear entirely, but Atlanta became one of the South's most racially progressive cities. African-Americans began playing major roles in Georgia's industrial and political arenas and a large number of African-American mayors and legislators now serve in the state's cities and towns.

Children at an Integrated School

Georgia Today

Today Georgia has one of the fastest-growing populations in the United States — in the ten years between 1980 and 1990 alone, its population grew by one million.

Atlanta is a booming city that is widely considered the cultural, transportation, and financial center of the South. Major international corporations, such as the Coca-Cola Company and the Cable News Network (CNN), have their headquarters in Atlanta. In 1988, Atlanta was the host city to the Democratic National Convention, and in 1996, the eyes of the world were on the city when the summer Olympic Games were held there. Atlanta's success has prompted many people to call Georgia "the Empire State of the South," a comparison to New York, which is nicknamed the Empire State.

Although agriculture isn't Georgia's major source of income anymore, farmers continue to raise cotton, tobacco, pecans, peanuts, peaches, and many other crops. Textile manufacturing is an important industry in Georgia, along with the production of automobiles, airplanes, and paper. Georgia's mild climate gives the state a year-round tourist season as well — more than thirty-two million tourists visit Georgia each year.

Some people come to see relics of the state's southern past, visiting antebellum sites in Athens, Wakinsville, Eatonton, and Macon, or strolling down Savannah's cobblestone streets among the city's carefully preserved buildings in the eighteenth-century Historic Landmark District. Georgia's hundred-mile-long eastern coastline contains the beautiful beaches of the Sea Islands. The majestic Blue Ridge Mountains near the northeastern border are part of the Appalachian range and are among the most spectacular natural spots in the state.

Coastal Georgia

Blue Ridge Mountains

Downtown Atlanta

Things to Do and Places to See

Callaway Gardens

Callaway Gardens is a 14,000-acre horticultural center located near the town of Pine Mountain in west-central Georgia. Visitors to the park can spend time in a tropical butterfly center with more than one thousand butterflies of fifty different species or try to identify some of the four hundred varieties of fruits, vegetables, and herbs in a seven-and-a-half-acre vegetable garden. More than five thousand varieties of native and hybrid azaleas and many different kinds of wildflowers can also be found in the gardens. Guests of the gardens can also go boating, hiking, golfing, and swimming.

Centennial Olympic Park

Centennial Olympic Park was built in 1996 as a central gathering place during the Atlanta Olympic Games. It is owned by the state of Georgia and is the largest new city park to be built in the United States in more than twenty years. A dramatic Fountain of

Rings marks the gateway to the park. Inside the park are twenty-four flags — twenty-three of the flags represent the host countries of the modern Olympic Games, and the twenty-fourth is the Olympic flag. The park is home to a one-hundred-year-old Georgia pecan tree and a 1,200-seat amphitheater where cultural events take place year-round.

The Chattahootchee Riverwalk

Columbus is a real, honest-to-goodness river town, located on the banks of the Chattahootchee River. The city's twelve-mile Riverwalk Park is the perfect place to bike, jog, or just stroll along the river. The Chattahootchee River is also home to the Chattahootchee Princess Riverboat, an authentic paddleboat from the 1880s.

Dahlonega Gold Museum

At the Dahlonega Gold Museum you can pan for gold just like the old Georgia miners. The museum displays real gold nuggets, along with the tools used by the miners during the gold rush. Take a pan and see if you can strike gold. You get to keep whatever you find!

Jekyll and Saint Simons Islands

These are just two of the many small islands lining Georgia's southeastern coast. Called the Golden Isles, they are part of the Sea Islands chain that continues across the border into Florida. Saint Simons Island is home to more than two hundred species of birds and was also the site of the Battle of the Bloody Marsh and Fort Frederica, one of the earliest forts constructed by James Oglethorpe. Jekyll Island was once a private resort where wealthy families, such as the Rockefellers, Morgans, and Vanderbilts, had summer homes. The homes are now open to visitors.

Jekyll Island

Saint Simons Island

Cannon at Kennesaw Mountain Park

Kennesaw Mountain National Battlefield Park

Located near Marietta, this park was the site of the Battle of Kennesaw Mountain between the troops of Union general William Tecumseh Sherman and the Confederate troops of General Joseph Johnson. The battle took place on June 27, 1864, and the losses on the Union side — more than two thousand — were the most severe suffered during the Georgia campaign.

Martin Luther King Jr. National Historic Site

This twenty-three-acre National Historic Site in downtown Atlanta includes the house where Dr. King was born, the Ebenezer Baptist Church where he and his father were both pastors, and the tomb where Dr. King is buried. The Freedom Hall complex houses the Martin Luther King Jr. Center for Social Change, founded by Dr. King's widow, Coretta Scott King.

Birthplace of Martin Luther King Jr.

Martin Luther King Jr.'s memorial tomb

Overview of Great Temple Mound

The Ocmulgee National Monument

This is the site of an ancient temple mound that belonged to Georgia's Creek tribe of Native Americans, located just outside Macon. Today, an archaeological museum displays Indian artifacts from the past ten thousand years.

Okefenokee Swamp

The Okefenokee Swamp National Wildlife Refuge

This freshwater wildlife refuge, the second largest in the nation, was established in 1937 to preserve the 438,000 acres of swampland located in Georgia and northern Florida. Visitors to the refuge are allowed to canoe, boat, and bike, but be careful — alligators and snakes live in the swamp, too.

Stone Mountain Memorial Park

This park is best known for the huge carving on the north side of Stone Mountain depicting the figures of Confederate leaders Jefferson Davis, Robert E. Lee, and Thomas "Stonewall" Jackson on horseback. The magnificent work of art is the world's largest carving on exposed granite. Sky rides to the mountain, evening laser shows, and a world-renowned golf course make this park one of Georgia's biggest attractions.

Carving of Confederate leaders on Stone Mountain

Famous People from Georgia

Martha McChesney Berry (1866–1942)

When Martha McChesney Berry was growing up near the small town of Rome, she had the best education money could buy. She knew, however, that many rural Georgian children were not so lucky, growing up poor and uneducated. As an adult, she became an educator and, with her own money, established schools for underprivileged children.

Jimmy Carter (1924–)

The thirty-ninth President of the United States was born in the town of Plains, the son of a peanut farmer. He grew up to become governor of Georgia, and eventually made his way to the White House in 1977.

His most important achievement as President came in 1979, when he helped negotiate a peace treaty between two longtime Middle Eastern enemies, Israel and Egypt.

Tyrus Raymond (Ty) Cobb (1886–1961)

When Ty Cobb was growing up in Narrows, his father felt that he spent far too much time playing baseball. All that playing paid off, though, when he became a major league player in 1905. "The Georgia Peach," as he was known, started out as an outfielder for the Detroit Tigers, and later played for the Philadelphia Athletics. Records he set include batting over .400 for three seasons, and over .300 in twenty-three seasons. No other player has beaten those records yet. In 1936, Ty Cobb was chosen as one of the first players inducted into the Baseball Hall of Fame.

Dr. Martin Luther King Jr. (1929–1968)

Perhaps no other civil rights leader in the history of America has done more to bring people of different races together than Dr. Martin Luther King Jr. of Atlanta. He devoted his entire life to the goal that every American be treated equally.

Dr. King believed in nonviolent civil disobedience as a form of protest. He first came to national attention when he organized a successful bus strike in the city of Montgomery, Alabama in 1955. Before the strike, state law decreed that blacks were supposed to sit in the back of the bus. At the urging of Dr. King and other activists, the blacks of Montgomery refused to ride on the buses until the laws were changed.

After the Montgomery bus strike, Dr. King became famous all over the country. In 1963, he gave his famous "I Have a Dream" speech during a march on Washington, D.C., expressing his hope that one day people would not be judged by the color of their skin. In 1964, for his work in the civil rights movement, he became the youngest person ever to win the Nobel Peace Prize.

Dr. King was assassinated in 1968. His birthday, in January, is now a federal holiday.

Juliette Gordon Low (1860–1927)

When Juliette Gordon Low was growing up in Savannah, she had so many interests she could hardly find time for them all. In addition to her love of camping and the outdoors, she loved to sketch, act, and write. When she grew up, she found a way to introduce all of her passions to girls across the United States by founding the Girl Scouts of America. She got the idea after meeting Lord Robert Baden-Powell, founder of the Boy Scouts in England. On March 12, 1912, eighteen girls from Savannah met to form the first Girl Scout troop in America. Today, the Girl Scouts have more than three million members across the United States.

Margaret Mitchell (1900–1949)

It's almost impossible to think of Georgia without thinking about Scarlett O'Hara and Rhett Butler. Vain, fearless Scarlett and romantic, roguish Rhett are the main characters of *Gone with the Wind,* the Pulitzer Prize–winning novel by Atlanta native Margaret Mitchell. The romance novel tells Scarlett and Rhett's love story against the background of the Civil War, describing in detail the destruction of Atlanta. Margaret Mitchell never published another book, but the well-loved *Gone with the Wind* is considered an American classic, as is the 1939 film it inspired. Margaret Mitchell's house on Peachtree Street in Atlanta is now a museum.

John Roosevelt (Jackie) Robinson (1919–1972)

Jackie Robinson was born in the town of Cairo to a family of sharecroppers. In 1945, when he first started playing baseball, there was a special league just for blacks called the Negro Leagues. In 1947, Jackie Robinson made history when he donned a Brooklyn Dodgers uniform and became the first African-American to play in the major leagues. That year he was also named National League Rookie of the Year. He had a career batting average of .311 and led the Dodgers to six World Series and one championship. In 1962 he was inducted into the Baseball Hall of Fame.

Ted Turner (1938–)

Broadcasting and entertainment executive Ted Turner started the twenty-four-hour news station CNN in Atlanta in 1980. After the success of that network, he went on to build a major media empire. His Turner Broadcasting System, the main company that runs all of his businesses (including the Atlanta Braves baseball team, the Atlanta Hawks basketball team, and several cable televi-sion networks) was combined with another company, Time Warner, in 1996. Early in the year 2000, Internet service company America Online agreed to buy Time Warner, making Ted Turner vice chairman of AOL Time Warner, now the world's largest media and entertainment company.

Alice Walker (1944–)

Civil rights activist, college professor, poet, and writer Alice Walker was born in Eatonton. She published her first story at the age of twenty-one and received a letter of encouragement from Langston Hughes, a famous African-American poet and writer.

Her novel *The Color Purple* won the Pulitzer Prize in 1983.

Letters from the Front

The 50th Regiment Georgia Volunteer Infantry was formed in March 1862. The infantry was made up mostly of local men from the Savannah area. One of those soldiers was John G. F. McCall.

These are excerpts from letters that John McCall wrote to his family during the Civil War. They give a firsthand account of what it was like to be a Confederate soldier.

Camp near Fredericksburg, Virginia
December 3rd, 1862
My Dear Sister,
As I have a few leisure moments to spend this lonesome evening I will decode them by answering your very kind and highly appreciated letter that came to hand yesterday, which afforded me great pleasure to peruse and also to hear that you are all well.
I haven't anything of a cheering nature to communicate to you.
Only times are very dull and hard here at the present. We are daily expecting a fight here, as we are a mile and half of the Yankees, supposed to be two hundred thousand. Our pickets stand on one side of the river and the Yankees on the other, not more than 100 yards apart. . . . It is getting very cold in this part of the country now and continues to get colder. I don't know what we will all do here this winter. The boys have nearly all drawn shoes, and are drawing some clothing occasionally, but not nearly enough to supply their wants. I am proud to know that the people of Brooks County have not forgotten the suffering soldiers who have rallied here in their defense as well as our own. I want to come home very bad, but I don't know when I will ever get the chance to come. . . . Give my love to all and accept this for yourself. I remain as ever your affectionate brother until death,
J. G. F. McCall

Camp near Fredericksburg, Virginia
April 22nd, 1863
Dear Father and Mother,
I again embrace the opportunity to answer your kind letter. I was glad to hear that all was well though sorry to hear that Pa had got his hand mashed. I want him to wear his whiskers til I come home and don't think that the time is a far distant, for I am of the opinion that this unholy war will come to a wind up before long. I think that the Yanks are getting very tired of it. General Longstreet gave them fits the other day at Suffolk. He took 600 prisoners and a large quantity of commissaries. . . .

25

There is a smart sickness now in camps but thank the Lord my health has been preserved so far. You need not be uneasy about my scarceness of money for if I need money I will be sure to let you know it. . . . I must close as I have not got time to [w]rite more as we are going to have general inspection today. Excuse my uninteresting letter, bad spelling and writing. I remain as ever
Your son,
J. G. F. McCall

This last letter is from John's cousin, William, to John's father.

Petersburg, Virginia
June 19th, 1864
My dear Uncle,
I have the painful news of writing you that Cousin John was killed a few minutes ago. He was detailed as sergeant of the Snapshooters and in looking over the breastworks he was shot through the top of the head. He lived a few minutes after he was shot, but was not able to speak after being hit. I shall have him buried as decently as possible. . . . Desperate as the time seems, it is an old saying that the darkest time is just before day. General Grant has succeeded in getting very close to Petersburg, but will have the same obstacle to meet with which he has met with for the past (nearly two months). I think we will have a desperate fight here in a day or two. . . . The Yankees are close enough to shell the town but General Beauregard has threatened them if they do it. . . .

I shall try to get a coffin to have cousin John buried. I do not know whether I can procure one or not. If it is a possible thing to do, so be assured that I will have it attended to. . . . All of his effects are here in the hands of Lt. Whittington. Nothing more at present. . . . No words of consolation can do much good, more than to say that John was universally liked by all who knew him.

Give my love to all and Aunt Vicey, Cousin Becca, and except a due portion for yourself.
Write soon,
Your obedient nephew,
W. C. McCall

Talking Leaves

For centuries, the elders of the Cherokee Nation passed along their knowledge of the past by telling stories to younger Cherokees. Theirs was an oral history, told in their native language from generation to generation. The Cherokee people had no written language, at least not until 1821, when a Cherokee named Sequoya created the Cherokee alphabet.

Sequoya was born in Tennessee, but he moved to Georgia when he was young, and learned to be a silversmith. Sequoya first came up with the idea for a Cherokee alphabet while visiting the home of his friend Charles Hicks, a wealthy Georgia farmer. George Hicks taught Sequoya how to write his name in English so that he could sign his work, just like the white silversmiths did.

Sequoya with his Cherokee alphabet

That one small good deed brought about a major change in the history of the Cherokee Nation. After learning to write his name in English, Sequoya became convinced that the Cherokee people needed to read and write in their own language.

At first, Sequoya tried to create pictograms that would represent entire sentences or thoughts. But he quickly came to the conclusion that such an alphabet could not work. Instead, he created an alphabet made up of 85 letters. Each letter represented a sound in the Cherokee oral language. He called the alphabet Talking Leaves. The Talking Leaves became the official written alphabet of the Cherokee Nation in 1821, twelve years after Sequoya began working on the project.

Sequoya's Talking Leaves not only gave the Cherokee Nation a way to record its history, it also provided the tools needed to create America's first Native-American-language newspaper, *The Cherokee Phoenix*. The first edition of this groundbreaking paper was published in 1828.

A Peach Treat from the Peach State

This yummy cupcake snack tastes best made with fresh Georgia peaches, but you can use canned peaches, too.

Peachy-Keen Cupcakes

Bake a batch of cupcakes using a white cake mix. Follow the directions on the box to be certain that your cupcakes come out perfectly. Make sure an adult puts the cupcakes in the oven. While the cupcakes are baking, create this peachy topping.

Topping ingredients:

1 cup sugar
1 tablespoon cornstarch
3 ounces peach Jell-O mix

1 cup water
4 cups thinly sliced peaches

Mix the sugar, cornstarch, Jell-O mix, and water in a medium saucepan. Ask an adult to cook the mixture over medium heat until thickened, stirring constantly. Stir in the sliced peaches.

Once your cupcakes are finished, ask an adult to remove them from the oven. Spoon the peach mixture over the warm cupcakes. Place them in the refrigerator to cool.

For extra sweetness, top your Peachy-Keen Cupcakes with whipped cream before serving.